Criminal Procedures: a Critique of the Court's Development, and the Application of the Bill of Rights

by

Edward E. Peoples, DPA

Instructor Emeritus

Administration of Justice Department

Santa Rosa Junior College

Distributed by

Meadow Crest Publishing

P. O. Box 1485, Forestville, CA 95436

Phone: (707) 887-1877. e-mail: Meadowcrestpublishing@msn.com

10 9 8 7 6 5 4 3 2 1

Copyright © and 2015 by Edward E. Peoples

ISBN# 978-0-9835049-3-1

NOTE: A substantial portion of this monograph was taken from the college text, *Criminal Procedures in California – 5th ed.*, by Edward E. Peoples

Criminal Procedures: a Critique of the Court's Development, and the Application of the Bill of Rights

Introduction

Criminal procedures are founded upon a trilogy that includes two legal concepts and a body of law that is as old as our independence and as sacred as our freedom. First, we have an **adversary system** in which two sides (the prosecutor and the defense) with fair and equal access to the same resources and information, compete in open court to arrive at the legal truth. Second, we use the absolute maximum degree of proof that humans are capable of having to convict a citizen of a crime, **proof beyond a reasonable doubt.**

Within this same conceptual framework, we use lesser degrees of proof when less serious intrusions into the freedom of citizens occur, such as reasonable suspicion and probable cause. Third, we have a body of law derived from our British legal heritage called **common law**; a body of law that was not written, but that has evolved over time in Great Britain through custom, tradition, and court decisions, rather than statutes. This became the law of the land in our early in British history and was the basis for much as the written law in America.

Many states no longer recognize any common law. Today, our laws are recorded in an array of books called **codes**, and are divided into categories, discussed below. If it is not written in some code, it is not the law. Nevertheless, the basis of the laws we follow today, as well as many appellate case decisions, comes from our common law heritage. However, our experiences with British law, both good and bad, strongly influenced what specific laws and legal safeguards our forefathers enacted.

The parts of this trilogy are bound together by a document that has become the ultimate source of all of our legal rights and wrongs, the **United States Constitution.** After the Revolutionary War, the states that had been formed united together under the Articles of Confederation, a document that loosely bound the states together, but that was totally inadequate in providing any viable structure to govern a nation. It was as if thirteen individual states were competing for the same things. A new form of government was needed.

Seventy-four men were selected from among the states to meet and amend the Articles. Fifty-five of those chosen delegates met in Philadelphia from May to mid-September 1787, and created a new document, a new structure that bound those states and all future states together under a strong central government – they created the **Constitution**.

It is that document that binds us together as a nation under law. The Constitution was signed by thirty-nine of the delegates and was finally ratified by a majority of the states in 1788, after negotiations in which the framers of the Constitution promised to add a Bill of Rights to the Constitution that would guarantee certain rights to the states and to all citizens. It went into effect on the first Wednesday in March 1789.

The reason that the Constitution is the ultimate source of our laws was summed up best in 1803 by Supreme Court Justice John Marshall when he stated that "*Any nation created by a document, must hold that document supreme.*"

For many years the rights guaranteed individuals in the Bill of rights only applied in federal proceedings. It took many years and the trials and tribulations of many criminal defendants to have these guarantees of the Bill of Rights apply at all levels of criminal proceedings for every individual.

This monograph first examines how the current structure we use in criminal proceedings developed over time. Next, we describe the process and court appellate cases that over time made the guarantees of the Fourth, Fifth, and Sixth Amendments binding on state criminal proceedings. A selected number of appellate court cases are cited and some are reviewed in detail. The reader may read these cases in their entirety by merely inserting the case citation in the search bar of a computer, ie. Breed v. Jones, 1999. The reasoning of the judges makes for interesting study.

A Brief History of Selected Procedures

The purpose here is not to provide an in-depth history lesson. Rather, it is to touch on the origins of selected procedures and processes that are used today and are important to know in appreciating why our current system operates as it does. Only those procedures that grew out of our British common law heritage are discussed. The focus is on certain aspects of procedural law and the court structure. Consequently, the history of law enforcement and police procedures is not addressed, other than that of the sheriff as his role relates to his court responsibilities.

Role of the Sheriff

After the fall of the Holy Roman Empire in 395 B.C., various tribes from the continent of Europe began settling Great Britain, primarily the Angles, Saxons, and Jutes. Their system of justice was tribal, had a high degree of citizen involvement, and emphasized restitution made directly to the victim of an offense. Eventually, these tribes merged into one large tribe, the Anglo-Saxons, and came to be ruled by Alfred the Great by about 870 A.D. For the first time, there was a King ruling the entire land and population of England. He began moving the justice system from a tribal and restitutional approach to a state run system in which the state was the victim of all crimes.

One of his first acts was to divide England into fifty-two political subdivisions called **shires**. Then, he appointed a knight to be his law enforcement agent in each shire. The term for "agent" was **Reeve**. Consequently, by this early date, we have a chief law enforcement officer in each shire, the Reeve. Now, if one were to say the two words together, faster and faster, while slurring slightly, it would come out as shire-reeve .... shire-eeve .... shireve .... sheriff .... sheriff .... **sheriff**.

The original responsibilities of the sheriff included enforcing the King's laws, arresting suspects, holding them for trial, and often acting as judge and executioner. Now, of course, other officials hold trial and carry out punishments, but the role of sheriff has otherwise changed very little in over a thousand years. As an aside, it is interesting to note that in England the sheriff dropped the judicial role in favor of law enforcement, and now the role is just an honorary title. In Scotland, however, the sheriff is a local judge, but has no police powers.

Early Methods of Trial

Before the development of the state under Alfred the Great, the Saxons and other tribes had a tribal court, described in our terms as a **Hundred Court** that included representatives from the various tribes and kin-groups living on lands divided into hundreds. Each hundred could support approximately 100 kin-groups. As the state evolved, the sheriff came to head this court, and eventually the King's Court, which he was responsible for forming and directing.

Early trial methods were swift and rather brutal. One such method, known as **trial by ordeal** required the accused to stand before the court and either hold his hands in a pot of boiling water or hold a hot iron or a hot rock for a few seconds. Then, his hands would be wrapped for two days. Upon the third day, the wraps would be removed and he would show his hands. If burn or scar marks showed, he was found guilty and killed because God had not intervened to remove the marks, as he would have with an innocent man.

A similar method used if the court was near some water was to have the accused swim with rocks tied to him, or to weigh him down with rocks, and throw him into the water. If he managed to swim free, in the first example, or if he managed to undo the rocks and survive, he was guilty because the devil had helped to set him free. One can imagine that the recidivist rate (rate of return to crime) was very low with these methods.

A less severe method, known as **compurgation**, required the accused to purge himself by swearing his innocence, with the support of witnesses, called **oath helpers**, to uphold his testimony. Interestingly enough, the number of oath helpers required was twelve. Another milder method was called **atonement**, which required the accused to pay compensation (restitution) to the victim. Initially, the amount atoned went to the victim. However, as the state assumed more control over the justice system, the amount was paid directly to the court.

This practice of atonement was also used extensively in the church courts, which were developing parallel to and in support of the king's courts. Atonement became a useful way of raising revenue. During this period, the sheriff presided over the courts and collected the compensation. Also, the Hundred Courts gave way to the practice of the sheriff convening the court, with twelve men sitting to represent the Hundred, or the citizens.

The Norman Conquest

The next significant development occurred in 1066. From 1042 to 1066, St. Edward, the Aetheling (the Confessor) was king of England. As he neared the end of his reign, disputes erupted over who would succeed him. He promised the crown to William, Duke of Normandy (in France). However, just before dying, he changed his mind and appointed a local knight, Harold of Wessox, as king. He was crowned on January 6, 1066. Duke William (aka **William the Conqueror**) thought the crown was rightfully his, so he landed his troops at Hastings, in southern England, on September 27, defeated Harold's army, and declared all of England his. William was crowned King of England on Christmas day in Westminster Abbey.

One of his first efforts to control the citizens was to replace all the Anglo-Saxon reeves (sheriffs) with his own Norman knights. He also redistributed much of the land to his knights. Consequently, his rule in general, and the Norman reeves in particular, was not well received. The people frequently hid men wanted by the sheriff, or helped them to escape after arrest and before trial.

In an effort to counter these reactions by the citizens, William initiated a procedure called **recognizance** (a French word) which required the accused, or his family, friends, or townspeople to post something of value in order to gain the freedom of the accused pending trial. Then, if they helped the accused escape, they would forfeit to the King what they had posted.

Today, we call this procedure posting **bail**, posting an amount of money with the court to gain the freedom of the accused, pending trial. In fact, today we have gone beyond having the accused post money, and in many cases allow the accused to post his or her word, or promise to return to court when required. We call this procedure releasing the accused on his or her **own recognizance**, or OR.

If the accused fails to appear, he or she can be charged with a new crime of failing to return, which can be either a felony or a misdemeanor, depending upon the level of the original crime charged. Think of it, the word and procedure known as recognizance has been a vital part of our justice system for over 935 years.

William also added **trial by battle** as a method of trial and settling disputes between individuals. However, the practice was limited to the Knights. Commoners continued to perform ordeals or pay atonement. As the king's power grew, so did that of the Church, and the Church made increasing use of atonement as the preferred method of making up for violating church laws, and for other sins.

The State Becomes the Victim

Until the beginning of the 12th century, victim **restitution** played an important role in settling disputes. The party wronged during the commission of a crime was considered the victim, deserving of compensation. That all changed when Henry I took the throne (1116-1132). He announced, "…that from now on the **King's Peace** shall be maintained throughout the kingdom…." Anyone who disturbs that peace by committing a crime was committing a crime against the king.

The king (state) became the victim of all crimes, and from that point until only recently, the real victim has been overlooked. The real victim suffered the loss from a crime, but the king reaped the rewards that came from a conviction.

King Henry also created **two crime categories**: He said, "There will be certain crimes against the King's peace that we will call **felonies**." These were arson, robbery, false coinage, and all crimes of violence. These felonies were punishable by death, and a person wanted for committing any of these crimes was declared an outlaw.

Anyone could kill an outlaw and claim the reward that might be offered. In both cases, death and outlawry, the accused was considered to be civilly dead. Accused persons ceased to have any legal life, which meant that they could not own property, will or inherit property, or perform any other act that required a legal existence. Once they suffered civil death, the king assumed title to all their property. This practice of declaring convicted felons civilly dead and stripping them of much of their civil rights, was practiced in California as late as the 1970s.

All the lesser crimes were called **misdemeanors** (mis-behaviors), punishable by atonement or corporal punishment. We no longer use corporal punishment, but we certainly use atonement, or a fine, for most misdemeanors, and imposing a fine is still a way for the State to raise money. Thus, consider the fact that the words we use today to classify two major crime categories are approximately 880 years old and that the basic behaviors of each category are about the same.

A Court Structure and Procedures Emerge

Under King Henry II (1154-1189), the King's court was centralized at Westminster, the country was divided into five **judicial districts**, and knights were appointed as **circuit-riding judges** to travel about the realm hearing cases. Initially, it was the sheriff's job to present the case in court. However, because the people had so long played a part in their own justice system, going back into the tribal days, and because they did not always trust the sheriff, pressure mounted from the people to play a more direct role. Consequently, by about 1176, when a person was accused of a crime, it became the sheriff's job to summon twelve knights from the shire and four from the town or village to hear a preliminary version of the case.

This group came to be known as the **grand jury**. The sheriff was responsible for presenting enough evidence to the grand jury to convince them that a crime really had occurred and that the evidence showed that the accused probably committed it. If the grand jury agreed, the accused was held for trial before the circuit-riding judge. Otherwise, the accused was allowed to go free. Consequently, when the judge arrived, he heard only those cases that had been screened by the grand jury in this preliminary type of hearing, which made better use of his time.

Today every case that is prosecuted in federal court goes through the same process. The grand jury is often used at the state level, particularly in the eastern states. In other states, such as California, the prosecutor has the option of using the grand jury, or a similar procedure that is detailed in a later chapter. The phrase **probable cause** is used today to describe these two aspects that at first the sheriff was, and now the prosecutor is, required to prove:

> ➢ that a crime occurred

> ➢ that the accused probably committed it

A **probable cause hearing** in court required in every felony case before the accused can be held for trial. The details of this are described in Chapter 8.

Common Law

There was little, if any, written law controlling crime and punishment in England. Customs and traditions evolved from tribal practices and blended with society's values at the time. Consequently, when judges arrived at a court, heard a case, and rendered a decision, they would follow the customs as much as possible and would write the decisions and their reasons for them in a book.

Thus, over time, a body of law developed based on custom and tradition and its application to a variety of situations by judges. We call this **common law** because it was commonly understood as the tradition and practice within the community, and judges commonly followed it in deciding cases.

The Doctrine of Precedent

As the decisions of judges grew in number, they provided a basis for deciding similar future cases. Judges could look back to see how a similar situation had been judged in the past and could follow the same line of thinking. Today, when a court reviews a case and makes a decision that can be used as an example for deciding similar future cases, the decision is called a **precedent**. The use of precedent setting cases as a reference for deciding future cases is known by the Latin phrase *stare decisis*, or the **Doctrine of Precedent**.

Today, when an appellate court makes a case decision about some police or trial procedure, it sets a precedent and establishes a procedural rule. It becomes the example against which procedures in future similar cases are decided.

As citizens demanded an increasing role in their justice system, the practice developed of using one group of citizens as the grand jury and a second group, composed of twelve citizens, as a petite, or **trial jury**. Initially, the trial jurors conducted their own investigations, as well as hearing evidence and giving a verdict. This led to injustices because the jurors would listen to rumors and hearsay evidence during their investigations. Eventually, they were restricted to hearing the evidence in court, and the evidence was presented by the sheriff. Eventually, another knight presented the evidence and the sheriff then merely provided law enforcement and court security.

In today's criminal proceedings, the sheriff still provides law enforcement and security in the courts, and an attorney from the district attorney's office presents the evidence, but the process is the same.

Defense Counsel

An accused (knight) could have the assistance of a fellow knight in presenting his defense, but only if the crime charged was a misdemeanor. For many years, the king had enough authority to prohibit the accused from having assistance in felony cases. Naturally, the king did not want an accused felon having help in his defense because the accused would have a better chance of not being convicted. Then, the king would lose out on obtaining the felon's property.

The Magna Carta

Henry II, and the subsequent kings, did not completely support the use of jury trials and, when possible, encouraged the sheriff to act as judge, jury, and executioner, making it easier for the kings to confiscate properties of convicted felons. One of the worst abusers was King John, who assumed the throne upon the death of his brother, Richard the Lion Hearted. He moved against commoner and noble alike. The nobles did not seem too concerned when the king abused the rights of a commoner, but when John began abusing their rights, they responded quickly to protect their interests.

On June 15, 1215, the nobles surrounded King John at a spot just north of Windsor Castle known as the Plains of Runnymead, placed their lances to his body and offered him a deal he could not refuse. They told John that if he signed the document they laid before him, they would not run him through with their lances. John signed the document, known as the **Magna Carta**, or Great Charter, which listed thirty-seven rights guaranteed to the citizens, primarily to the nobles and the Church.

Actually, much of the Magna Carta was copied from an earlier document of Henry I, titled the *Charter of Liberties*, but the *Magna Carta* is the document remembered and cited as the main source of our **Bill of Rights**.

One of the principle rights guaranteed in the *Magna Carta* stated that **no free man would be seized or imprisoned, or deprived of his property, without first having the case reviewed and judged by his peers**. At the time, those guarantees referred only to those citizens (peers) to be chosen from the community to form the grand jury to review the evidence and determine if the case should go to trial.

That initial guarantee was interpreted broadly to form the basis of our constitutional due process, and was expanded in the U. S. Constitution to include the right to both the grand jury and the trial jury of one's peers.

A Court Structure is Completed

By the end of the 14th century, the use of the jury system was fairly well established. By about 1300, the role of **coroner** was created. A knight was appointed in each shire to view dead bodies before burial and investigate suspicious deaths to determine the cause; to list all the property of the deceased; to record the names of those felons convicted or declared outlaws; and to list and confiscate their property for the king. A coroner performs very similar responsibilities today in each county.

By the 1400s, society had grown more complex, with a larger population, more crime, and more cases to hear. The circuit-riding judges could no longer hear all the cases. Consequently, England was divided into five judicial districts, with a Crown Court in each district where the judges sat and heard cases. The **Peace Knight Act** of 1361 authorized the appointments of peace knights in the various cities and towns to hear the misdemeanor cases, while the felony cases went to the district Crown Courts.

Felony cases were first screened by the peace knight and grand jury at the local level, so that only those cases with sufficient evidence to show that a crime had occurred and that the accused had probably done, went on to trial. In felony cases, this amounted to a **probable cause hearing** before the Peace Knight in a lower court, after which the lower court judge, the Peace Knight, would either find that probable cause existed and refer the case to the district Crown Court for trial, or that probable cause was lacking and dismiss the case.

By the end of the 14th century there was a chief law enforcement officer for each county, who also detained prisoners and provided court security; a coroner; a body of law; an adversary system; the use of both prosecution and defense; a two-tier court structure; a jury system; the basic crime categories of felony and misdemeanor; the state as the victim of all crimes; the procedure of recognizance, or bail; and the principle of *stare decisis*, or precedent, which provides stability, predictability and fairness in the application of the law.

The point of this short history lesson is to show that the foundation and structure of our current system of justice was well established over 600 years ago. What has developed beyond that has increased the complexity of justice, but in many ways might be viewed as being more cosmetic than substantive.

Now we take a quantum leap from the 14th century to the present. First we need to bridge that 600-year gap with a look at the one essential link with the past that had the most significant impact on our procedural law, the *Magna Carta*. This document, and its predecessor, the *Charter of Liberties*, hold for us the essence of the rights of all people, and the guarantee of due process and the equal protection that are found in the **Bill of Rights**, the first ten Amendments to the Constitution.

The Bill of Rights - 1791

The federal document called the **Bill of Rights** contains the first ten Amendments to the United States **Constitution**. By including these in the Constitution, the Founding Fathers intended to guarantee certain rights for all the people in their dealings with the federal government. They did this because they thought the English king and his agents frequently had abused their rights when America was a colony. They wanted to be certain that these rights had complete protection under the new form of government. They also wanted to guarantee complete freedom of religion. Consequently, no religious tests are required to participate in government and God was not referred to in the Constitution.

Additional Amendments have been added to the Constitution over the years, and all of them are equally important. However, for our purposes in studying criminal procedures in this limited scope, only the following three Amendments will be examined: the Fourth, Fifth, and Sixth Amendments. They form the basis of most criminal procedures that we will study.

The Sixth and Eighth Amendments are equally important, but the critique of them would be studies by themselves.

➤ **Fourth Amendment**

The right of the people to be secure in their persons, houses, papers, and effects, against **unreasonable searches and seizures**, shall not be violated, and no warrants shall issue, but upon **probable cause**, supported by Oath or affirmation, and particularly describing the place to be searched, and the persons or things to be seized.

➤ **Fifth Amendment**

No person shall be held to answer for a capital, or otherwise infamous crime, unless on a presentment or indictment of a **Grand Jury**, except in cases arising in the land or naval forces, or in the militia, when in actual service in time of war or public danger; nor shall any person be subject to the same offense to be twice put in jeopardy of life or limb; nor shall be compelled in any criminal case to be a **witness against himself**, nor be deprived of life, liberty, or property, without due process of law; nor shall private property be taken for public use, without just compensation.

➤ **Fourteenth Amendment**

All persons born or naturalized in the United States, and subject to the jurisdiction thereof, are citizens of the United States and of the State wherein they reside. **No State shall make or enforce any law which shall abridge the privileges or immunities** of citizens of the United States; nor shall any State deprive any person of life, liberty, or property, without **due process of**

law; nor deny to any person within its jurisdiction the **equal protection** of the laws. (Added July 28, 1868)

Note that the Fourteenth Amendment was added seventy-seven years after the original Bill of Rights was written. This addition was necessary to ensure that no one violated the other Amendments. It has been used often by appellate courts as the basis for forcing states to comply with the other Amendments, because most states would not otherwise follow them, nor would they all enact their own laws to ensure those same rights. By using the fourteenth Amendment to make all the rights binding on the states, the Supreme Court standardized justice, in a sense, by insuring that all guarantees of the Bill of Rights would be applied equally everywhere. At least that is the theory.

In our study of the procedural rights guaranteed in these Amendments we examine two procedural rules derived from decisions of the U.S. Supreme Court: the **Exclusionary Rule** and the **Miranda Warning**. The two are blended together as procedural safeguards. They are procedural rules that an officer must be conscious of in every arrest and investigative situation that might involve a confession or the collection of other evidence. Every prosecutor and every defense attorney know the rules well and the defense will use them in almost every criminal case to defend a client's rights by excluding a confession or other evidence that were seized illegally, and/or the denial of a suspects right to an attorney.

Usually, when a police officer is subpoenaed to testify in court, it is to testify about how he or she obtained the evidence or confession, not about the guilt of the accused. The story of how this procedure was created, how it became a binding rule for every police officer to follow, and how exceptions to it have been allowed, will be presented below in detail as a prelude to studying police procedures.

The Exclusionary Rule and Fourth Amendment Protections

The role of an appellate courts, including the Supreme Court, is not to make law, but to interpret existing law. Specifically, the U. S. Supreme Court has the responsibility of interpreting what the U. S. Constitution means, and whether any state or federal law conflicts with the rights therein guaranteed to the people.

The Exclusionary Rule, however, was not created to clarify the constitution, but to control the conduct of police in their search for evidence of a crime because the U. S. Supreme Court, the Warren Court, did not trust the police to control their own conduct within the spirit of the Fourth Amendment.

Simply stated, the **Exclusionary Rule** is a rule of law which holds that:

> ➤ *evidence seized illegally by the government (law enforcement) is inadmissible in a court of law to prove guilt*

Obviously, police need to follow this rule to the letter. If they do not follow it, and seize evidence illegally, it cannot be used against the person arrested by the police and accused of the crime. This will result in the **suppression of evidence**. Without the evidence of a crime, the state cannot prove that a crime occurred, and the suspect will go free. One would think, then, that police would never seize evidence illegally because it would ruin their own case, and their efforts would be in vain.

There are certain guidelines for police to follow, but there is no absolute rule to govern every situation. Consequently, whether evidence is admitted or excluded from a trial depends on how judges interpret the general guidelines as applied to the situation before them. A judge of a higher court might disagree with the trial judge, and a judge at an even higher court might disagree with the other judge, and so on.

Sometimes it takes two or three years in this appellate process for the police officer to know whether the manner in which the evidence was seized was legal. Even in the U. S. Supreme Court, where nine justices sit as the highest legal authorities in the country, disagreement frequently occurs. However, their decision, possibly made by a vote of five to four, will become the law of the land.

Cases that Created the Exclusionary Rule

The Exclusionary Rule was created over time by case decisions of the U. S. Supreme Court by judging police behavior against the rights guaranteed in the Fourth Amendment. Initially, the court established what was known as the **Weeks Doctrine** by ruling that the Fourth Amendment only applied to federal procedures (***Weeks v. United States, 1914***). Several states followed the federal example and enacted their own similar procedures.

In another case, a Denver physician was charged with conspiring to perform an illegal abortion. He was convicted and sentenced to prison, but appealed on the basis of the Fourth Amendment in that the evidence was seized illegally. The U. S. Supreme Court, by a vote of six to three, referring to precedent set by the Weeks case ruled again that the Fourth Amendment only applied to federal procedures (***Wolf v. Colorado, 1949***).

Finally, one case stands as a watershed in the history of criminal due process and Fourth Amendment protection, Mapp ***v. Ohio, 1961***. It established one of the most controversial procedures of our time, the **Exclusionary Rule**, as a **mandatory procedure for all states**. It is revered by defense attorneys and reviled by some law enforcement officers. The case is important enough in the study of criminal procedures to describe it in some detail.

At about 2:30 a.m. on May 20, 1957, a Cleveland police sergeant, Carl Delau, arrived home "a little drunk" from a party and went to bed. Shortly thereafter, he was awakened by a phone call from a man known to him as Don King, a reputed numbers racketeer (Roth wax, 1996). King told the sleepy Delau that someone had just bombed his house and wanted to know what to do. DeLau asked how he knew it was actually a bomb, and King replied that his entire front porch and front wall had been blown off. Apparently, Delau indicated that he would report it. Within a few minutes, however, the police dispatcher phoned Delau and told him to "get out there" to investigate a bombing.

Three days later, Sgt. DeLau received a phone tip that the alleged bomber, Virgil Ogiltree, was hiding out at a house in Cleveland. That afternoon, Sgt. DeLau and two other detectives went to the address, a two-story, two-family flat, identified Ogiltree's car parked near the residence, and staked it out. Finally, the officers got tired of waiting, so they went to the door of the flat occupied by a young black woman, Dollree Mapp, who was known to DeLau from a prior arrest. They knocked on the door, and she called down from the upstairs window to ask what they wanted. When they told her they wanted to search her house, she said she would call her attorney first, and disappeared from the window. She returned within a few minutes and told DeLau that they could not search without a warrant.

Sgt. DeLau and the two other detectives returned to their car and radioed in for a warrant and for some additional officers to help. Three hours later they returned to Miss Mapp's residence, along with six uniformed officers, and again asked Miss Mapp's permission to search, claiming that they had a warrant. When she refused, one officer broke a door windowpane, unlatched the door, and they all entered the hallway, moving toward her flat. She rushed down to meet them and demanded to see the warrant. When one officer held up a piece of paper, claiming it was the warrant, she grabbed it out of his hand and shoved it down inside the front of her sweater.

Stories about what occurred next vary. According to Sgt. DeLau, the warrant was visible, protruding from her sweater, so he grabbed it back. She then became unruly and had to be restrained with handcuffs. According to Miss Mapp, the officers handcuffed her, held her in a corner, and then reached into her bosom after the warrant.

Regardless of who is correct, the police obtained the piece of paper they claimed was the warrant, cuffed her, and thoroughly searched her residence, including drawers, closets and cabinets. Ogiltree, the bombing suspect was not found because he was not there. However, the police did find pictures of both male and female nude models with all their organs totally undressed, some pencil sketches of nudes, and four books: *London Stage Affair*, *Affairs of a Troubadour*, *Memoirs of a Hotel Man*, and *Little Darlings*.

Police also searched her basement and found illegal gambling material. She was arrested and charged both with possession of the betting material, a misdemeanor, and possession of obscene materials, a felony. On their way out, police also searched the apartment next to Mapp's, where they did find Ogiltree hiding, and they arrested him for the bombing.

Miss Mapp was tried on the misdemeanor in Police Court and was acquitted. Her felony trial began in September 1958, and she was charged with "...unlawfully and knowingly having in her possession certain lewd and lascivious books, pictures, and photographs."

Her attorney questioned the legality of the search, and when police indicated that the so-called warrant had disappeared, he moved to suppress the evidence, claiming that the officers actually did not have a warrant. Apparently, no one brought up the fact that even if the police did have a real warrant, it would not have mentioned any "obscene" material.

The trial judge denied the motion to suppress, and Mapp was convicted and sentenced to seven years in prison - seven years for possession of so-called obscene material in her own home. Her attorney appealed to the Ohio State Supreme Court on the basis that the Ohio obscenity statute violated the First Amendment and, therefore, was unconstitutional. Four of the Ohio justices agreed, but their votes were not enough to reverse her conviction. Upon further appeal, the U. S. Supreme Court agreed to hear the case in 1961.

NOTE: The basis of the appeal by her attorney centered on the constitutionality of Ohio's broadly worded obscenity statute and Mapp's First Amendment right to free expression, and the right to possess any written materials or drawings in the privacy of her own home. Her attorney did not make this a Fourth Amendment search and seizure issue. Many of the questions raised by the justices during the oral argument by the state's attorney were only about the fact that mere possession of obscenity in one's own home was a felony. The justices seemed to have a real concern about criminalizing that sort of private behavior.

When Mapp's attorney attempted to explain that the so-called obscene material did not even belong to her, but to a former roomer, Justice Felix Frankfurter interrupted to ask just exactly what the issue was before the court, and asked if it included the legality of the search and seizure.   Her attorney seemed somewhat flustered by the mention of this new issue. Nevertheless, he did start to argue that it was illegal, when Justice Frankfurter interrupted him again to say "Are you asking us to overrule the *Wolf* case in this court? I notice it isn't cited in your brief." Mapp's attorney was not familiar with the *Wolf* case, and perhaps not even familiar with search and seizure issues, so he indicated no, that he was not asking the court to reverse *Wolf*, and he let the issue of search and seizure drop.

Upon completion of the oral arguments by both sides, an unusual event occurred.   For the first time in the court's history, it allowed an oral argument to be presented by a representative of the American Civil Liberties Union (ACLU) who had submitted a written brief and requested to be heard as *Amicus curiae*, a friend of the court.

The ACLU attorney seemed to sense that Justice Frankfurter wanted to make an issue out of the search and seizure by bringing it up himself, so the ACLU attorney began his address to the court by referring to the *Wolf* case and stated:

> …we are asking this court to reconsider *Wolf v. Colorado* and to find that evidence that is unlawfully and illegally obtained should not be permitted into a state proceeding and its production is a violation of the federal constitution's Fourth Amendment and the Fourteenth Amendment. We have no hesitancy in asking the court to reconsider it because we think that it is a necessary part of due process.

After stating this, however, the attorney indicated that his primary purpose in addressing the court was to urge them to declare the obscenity statute of Ohio unconstitutional, and he proceeded to address that statute as a First Amendment issue in the Mapp case.

Later, in the privacy of their chambers, the Justices discussed the legality of Ohio's obscenity statute within the context of the First and Fourteenth Amendments, and they unanimously voted to reverse Mapp's conviction and declare the obscenity statute unconstitutional (Rothwax, 1996). Justice Tom Clark was assigned to write the court's opinion. However, the opinion he wrote focused on the Fourth Amendment and the Exclusionary Rule and did not address the obscenity issue or the Ohio statute at all.

When his opinion was circulated among the other Justices to read and sign, Justice Potter Stewart was "shocked" by the change in the written opinion from that which had been accepted as the basis for reversal of Mapp's conviction. As Judge Harold J. Rothwax stated, Justice Clark's opinion "…was based on arguments that had never even been briefed, argued, or discussed before the court (Rothwax, 1996, p. 45)."

Justice Stewart later indicated that he believed the other Justices met together to form a "rump caucus" and agreed to make the Mapp case a vehicle by which the Fourteenth Amendment could be used to make the Fourth Amendment and the Exclusionary Rule binding on the states.

Regardless of the objections of Justice Stewart and several other Justices, the opinion written by Justice Clark was approved by a **five to four majority** (the Warren Court, with its due process orientation) and held that:

> ...the Fourth Amendment's right of privacy has been declared enforceable against the States through the Due Process Clause of the Fourteenth, it is enforceable against them by the same sanction of exclusion as is used against the Federal Government. Were it otherwise, then, just as without the *Weeks* rule the assurance against unreasonable federal searches and seizures would be "a form of words," valueless and undeserving of mention in a perpetual charter of inestimable human liberties, so too, without that rule, the freedom from state invasions of privacy would be so ephemeral and so neatly severed from its conceptual nexus with the freedom from all brutish means of coercing evidence as not to merit this Court's high regard as a freedom implicit in the concept of ordered liberty.

With this decision, **the Exclusionary Rule was imposed on the states** and on all state and local law enforcement officers as the primary procedural law that guides their actions. It is against this rule that many of the efforts by police are judged legal or illegal. Any evidence seized illegally, in violation of the Fourth

Amendment, cannot be used in court to prove guilt. **The sole purpose of the rule is to police the police**; to deter police from violating the rights of citizens guaranteed in the Fourth Amendment.

The theory believed by the Court was that if the police know their evidence cannot be used if they seize it illegally, they will follow the law. It is a rule of law that demonstrates just how delicate the balance is between individual freedom and social protection, and how a simple majority of the Court can decide just where that balancing point will be.

One of the Supreme Court bailiffs in the Mapp case had agreed to phone Dollree Mapp when the Justices reached their decision. He phoned her every Monday morning for twelve weeks after her case was argued to say that no decision had been made. But, finally, on the thirteenth Monday he called her with the decision and, according to her, "...that was the day that the Supreme Court washed my conviction down the drain."

Dollree Mapp is all but forgotten by most people, but the rule that the Justices created from her case remains on the minds of every law enforcement officer, every attorney, and every judge, every day.

By way of conclusion, Dollree Mapp did not live happily ever after when her conviction was reversed. She was convicted of drug possession in New York in 1973, and was sentenced to a term in state prison of from twenty years to life. After serving nine years, four months and seventeen days in prison, her sentence was commuted to time served and she was paroled. She continued to maintain her innocence of the drug charge and petitioned the governor for a full pardon. After her release, she went to work in Long Island as a legal aid for prison inmates.

As for Don King, who had his front porch and front wall blown away by the bomb, he went on to become one of the country's leading boxing promoters. Sgt. DeLau eventually retired.

Exceptions to the Exclusionary Rule

As the saying goes, for every rule there are many exceptions. This is true for the Exclusionary Rule, and the Supreme Court has established three exceptions that affect the application of the rule by police in their collection of evidence:

> ➤ **inevitable discovery** exception
> ➤ **public safety** exception

> ➤ **good faith** exception

Each exception was created from one or more of the case decisions described below.

The Inevitable Discovery Exception

The inevitable discovery rule became a procedural law of the land, binding on all the states. It is a rule that means, in essence, that if police obtain evidence in violation of the Fourth Amendment, but they can prove by a **preponderance of the evidence** (fifty-one percent) that their evidence would have been found in the same condition anyway, by some legal means or independent source, it is admissible in court, and the Exclusionary Rule does not apply (see *State v. Williams,* **1970**, *Brewer v. Williams,* 1977, and *Nix v. Williams,* **1984**).

Williams was the defendant in this case and the original offense occurred in December 1968, when he kidnapped and killed a young girl. The evidence was initially ruled inadmissible because the trial court believed that the evidence (the girl's body and defendant's blanket) were obtained in violation of the Fourth Amendment.

The prosecutor appealed and thereafter, the case progressed slowly up the appellate ladder. The evidence was finally admitted in 1984, because the Supreme Court held that given the nature of the situation and the totality of circumstance surrounding the search for the girl, the evidence would have been found inevitably, Williams was convicted. The complexity of the *Williams* case was exceeded only by the length of time necessary to complete it. Think how long it took for this case to bring closure for the victim's family, if closure for such an act is ever possible.

The Public Safety Exception

On September 11, 1980, at approximately 12:30 am, Officer Frank Kraft was on road patrol in Queens, New York when a young woman approached his car. She told him that she had just been raped by a black male, approximately six feet tall, who was wearing a black jacket with the name "Big Ben" printed in yellow letters on the back. She told the officers that the man had just entered an A & P supermarket located nearby, and that the man was carrying a gun.

Once in the store, Officer Kraft spotted the suspect, who matched the description given by the woman, approaching a checkout counter. He apparently saw the officer, and turned and ran toward the rear of the store. Officer Kraft pursued him with a drawn gun, but lost sight of him for several seconds. Upon locating the suspect again, the officer ordered him to stop and put his hands over his head.

After handcuffing him, Officer Kraft asked him where the gun was, and the suspect nodded in the direction of some empty cartons and responded, "The gun is over there." Officer Kraft retrieved a loaded .38-caliber revolver from one of the cartons, formally placed the suspect under arrest, and then read him his *Miranda* rights from a printed card. The suspect, identified as Benjamin Quarles, indicated that he would be willing to answer questions without an attorney present. Officer Kraft then asked Quarles if he owned the gun and where he had purchased it. Quarles answered that it was his gun and that he had purchased it in Miami, Florida.

Quarles was charged with criminal possession of a weapon, but the judge excluded the gun and the statement, "The gun is over there," because the officer had not given Quarles the required *Miranda* warning before asking him where the gun was. The judge excluded the other statements as well because they were tainted by the initial procedural violation by the officer and became **fruits of the poison tree of evidence**.

The Appellate Division of the Supreme Court of New York affirmed the trial judge's decision. On appeal by the State, the U. S. Supreme Court, agreed to hear the case. It was argued in January 1984 and decided in June 1984. In the Court's opinion, Justice Rehnquist stated that:

> The Fifth Amendment guarantees that "no person...shall be compelled in any criminal case to be a witness against himself." However, ..."there is a **"public safety" exception** to the requirement that *Miranda* warnings be given before a suspect's answers may be admitted into evidence... and that the availability of that exception does not depend upon the motivation of the individual officers involved....Undoubtedly most police officers, if placed in Officer Kraft's position, would act out of a host of different, instinctive, and largely unverifiable motives - their own safety, the safety of others....Whatever the motivation of individual officers in such a situation, we do not believe that the doctrinal underpinnings of *Miranda* require that it be applied in all its rigor to a situation in which police officers ask questions reasonably prompted by a concern for the public safety....So long as the gun was concealed somewhere in the supermarket, with its actual whereabouts unknown, it obviously posed more than one **danger to the public safety**...We

conclude that the need for answers to questions in a situation posing a threat to the public safety outweighs the need for the...rule protecting the Fifth Amendment's privilege against self-incrimination.

From this abbreviated version of the court's opinion, it is obvious that the **justices were balancing the needs** of society for safety with the rights of the individual, Quarles. This public safety exception to the Exclusionary Rule shows that in the court's mind, **public safety comes first**.

It applies equally as well to **officer safety**, **victim safety**, and **suspect safety** (*U. S. v. Brady,* **1987**; *U. S. v. DeSantis,* **1989**; and *U. S. v. Carrillo,* **1994**), and particularly to the admissibility of statements taken without a *Miranda* admonition in an effort to ensure these safeties.

The Good Faith Exception

On the basis of a search warrant, an officer searched the suspect's (Leon) residence and found large quantities of drugs. The suspect was arrested and charged with conspiracy to possess and distribute a variety of drugs. At a suppression hearing, the judge concluded that the original search warrant had been issued without sufficient cause and dismissed the charges.

On appeal, the U. S. Supreme Court held that the search was legal and that the arresting officer should not be punished by having the evidence excluded when he acted in good faith. After a lengthy discussion, Supreme Court Justice White described the situation and delivered the opinion of the Court in *U. S. v. Leon,* **1984**.

This case presents the question whether the Fourth Amendment exclusionary rule should be modified so as not to bar the use in the prosecution's case-in-chief of evidence obtained by officers acting in reasonable reliance on a search warrant issued by a detached and neutral magistrate but ultimately found to be unsupported by probable cause...As yet, we have not recognized any form of good faith exception to the Fourth Amendment exclusionary rule... But the balancing approach that has evolved during the years of experience with the rule provides strong support for the modification currently urged upon us. As we discuss below...the costs and benefits of suppressing reliable physical evidence seized by officers reasonably relying on a warrant issued by a detached and neutral magistrate leads to the conclusion that such evidence should be admissible in the prosecution's case...the officers' reliance on the magistrate's determination of probable cause was objectively reasonable... (and the evidence is admissible).

Thus, the third exception to the Exclusionary Rule, the *Good Faith Exception* was created by case law by the Supreme Court with a majority of Justices favoring **public safety and law enforcement above the individual freedom** of a suspected law violator. Their decision has been reaffirmed in many subsequent cases (***U. S. v. McLaughlin,* 1988**; ***Illinois v. Krull,* 1987**; and ***Arizona v. Evans,* 1996**, to name but a few).

The Miranda Warning and the Right to Counsel

This portion of the chapter deals exclusively with the *Miranda* decision and the effect that it has on police procedures. The *Miranda* decision ranks alongside the *Mapp* and *Gideon* decisions as one of the three most significant precedent-setting cases in the history of procedural due process.

Most people take it for granted today that police comply with the requirements of *Miranda*, and that they have always done so. However, it took many years and several appellate decisions to achieve the full due process that suspects now enjoy when being questioned by law enforcement. Consequently, before examining *Miranda*, it will be useful to review a summary of the important cases leading up to the 1966 decision.

Later on in the chapter, the use of what is called the *Beheler Admonition* is presented as a current method used by police to avoid having to advise a suspect of any rights.

Forerunners to *Miranda*

Prior to the *Miranda* decision, the criteria for determining the admissibility of a confession in court was whether it had been given *freely and voluntarily*. Those terms are rather vague and leave much to interpretation. There were many efforts to change that standard and three cases stand out as forerunners to the current standard, as spelled out in *Miranda*. Two of these are examples of how the U. S. Supreme Court avoided dealing with the issue of confessions obtained by police interrogation, and one case shows the result of making a decision without including any method to enforce it.

The Prompt Arraignment Cases

The first case is ***McNabb v. U. S., 1943***, in which two McNabb brothers were convicted of killing a federal revenue agent during a raid on their family's still in the mountains near Chattanooga, Tennessee. They were arrested during the raid, then locked in a strip cell for over 14 hours, then interrogated continuously over the next two days.

They finally confessed, were convicted on the basis of their confession, and were sentenced to forty-five years in prison. On appeal, the U.S. Supreme Court refused to address the legality of their confession, and instead, used the federal arraignment rule, *Rule 5a* of the *Federal Rules of Criminal Procedures*, to reverse the McNabb convictions. This rule required **prompt arraignment** after arrest. The court did not want to establish any precedent on custodial interrogation.

In the second case, ***Mallory v. U. S., 1957***, the 19-year old Mallory, a man of limited intelligence (Robin, 1987, p. 171), was arrested by police in Washington D. C. on a charge of rape, a capital offense at the time. He was interrogated at the police station by a polygraph operator and a detective for over ten hours. He finally confessed, was convicted on the basis of his confession, and was sentenced to be executed.

On appeal, the U.S. Supreme Court again refused to deal with the legality of the confession. The court again used the federal rule, *Rule 5a*, to reverse his conviction, holding that Mallory had not been promptly arraigned.

The real significance of these two cases, aside from requiring prompt arraignment, is the fact that **no precedent was set in the area of illegal confessions**. The court had opportunities to address the issue, but declined to do so. There was a strong belief at the time that the U. S. Constitution was a federal document and the rights guaranteed therein applied only to federal proceedings. There was an equally strong belief that the states should be free to determine their own laws and justice system procedures. **States' rights** was a popular, almost sacred theme throughout the nation.

The On-the-Spot Counsel Case

On the night of January 19, 1960, Danny Escobedo's brother-in-law was fatally shot, and Danny was the prime suspect.   He was arrested without a warrant in the early hours of the next morning, and was interrogated at police headquarters.

He made no statement to the police, and was released late that afternoon after his attorney obtained a writ of *habeas corpus*, an order stating that he was being held illegally.

On January 30, Danny and his sister, now the widow of the deceased, were arrested and taken to police headquarters. Danny was handcuffed in the back of the police car on the way to the police station, when one of the arresting officers told him that a co-defendant had named him as the one who shot the deceased. According to Escobedo's later testimony, the detective also said, "They had us pretty well, up pretty tight, and we might as well admit to this crime," and that (Escobedo) replied, "I am sorry, but I would like to have advice from my lawyer." A police officer testified that, although Escobedo was not formally charged, "he was in custody" and "couldn't walk out the door."

Actually, Escobedo had been told that if he confessed and named the co-defendant as the shooter, he would be given immunity from prosecution and could go home. He confessed, and was detained, and charged with the murder.

At the trial, Escobedo's attorney made a motion to suppress the confession on the grounds that it had been obtained in violation of Escobedo's Sixth Amendment right to counsel. The trial judge denied the motion, and Escobedo was convicted.

The case was appealed to the U. S. Supreme Court, a court that now had a different composition than the earlier *McNabb* or *Mallory* Courts. This was the **Warren Court**, and it had a decidedly due-process orientation. In its decision (***Escobedo v. Illinois**, 1964*), the court held that:

> Under the circumstances of this case, where a police investigation is no longer a general inquiry into an unsolved crime but has begun to focus on a particular suspect in police custody who has been refused an opportunity to consult with his counsel and who has not been warned of his constitutional right to keep silent, the accused has been denied the assistance of counsel in violation of the Sixth and Fourteenth Amendments, and no statement extracted by the police during the interrogation may be used against him at a trial.

The court thought that its decision provided suspects with the constitutional guarantees in the Sixth Amendment. When a person became the focus of an investigation and was a suspect, and requested to speak with an attorney, the questioning had to stop. However, the decision lacked any provision for determining when the police investigation made the shift from a "...general inquiry into an unsolved crime but has begun to focus on a particular suspect in police custody...." Also, the police were not required to tell the person he or she was the suspect nor advise him or her of the right to speak with an attorney. Consequently, the decision requiring **on-the-spot counsel** after police made that *shift* had little, if any, effect on police procedures.

It was business as usual in many law enforcement agencies, and police continued to offer confessions as evidence if they were given freely and voluntarily.

The *Miranda* Case

The *Miranda* warning was named after the 1966 U. S. Supreme Court decision in which the 1963 conviction of Ernesto Miranda was reversed because the Court believed that he was deprived of his constitutional right to remain silent when questioned by police. The decision was one of the most important cases ever to come out of the Supreme Court. It is one that has often frustrated law enforcement, and one that often has been misunderstood. What follows below is an explanation that, hopefully, will clarify exactly what *Miranda* is, and when it **is** and **is not** necessary for police to give the admonition to a suspect in a criminal case.

Miranda v. Arizona, 1966

Ernesto Miranda, a 23-year old man of Mexican descent, was arrested at his home on March 13, 1963, and taken to the Phoenix Police Station, where he was placed in a lineup. He was immediately identified by a woman as the man who had kidnapped and raped her. He was taken into an interrogation room and questioned for two hours, after which he signed a confession to both crimes. His confession was admitted into evidence at his trial, over objections by his attorney, and he was found guilty of both charges. Miranda was sentenced to two concurrent terms of twenty to thirty years. On appeal, the U. S. Supreme Court held that:

..the prosecution may not use statements...stemming from **custodial interrogation** of the defendant unless it demonstrates the use of procedural safeguards effective to secure the privilege against self-incrimination. By **custodial interrogation, we mean questioning initiated by law enforcement officers after a person has been taken into custody or otherwise deprived of his freedom of**

action in any significant way. As for the procedural safeguards to be employed, unless other fully effective means are devised to inform accused persons of their right of silence and to assure a continuous opportunity to exercise it, the following measures are required.

Prior to any questioning, the person must be warned that he has a right to remain silent, that any statement he does make may be used as evidence against him, and that he has a right to the presence of an attorney, either retained or appointed.

The defendant may waive effectuation of these rights, provided the waiver is made voluntarily, knowingly and intelligently. If, however, he indicates in any manner and at any stage of the process that he wishes to consult with an attorney before speaking, there can be no questioning. Likewise, **if the individual is alone and indicates in any manner that he does not wish to be interrogated, the police may not question him**. The mere fact that he may have answered some questions or volunteered some statements on his own does not deprive him of the right to refrain from answering any further inquiries until he has consulted with an attorney and thereafter consents to be questioned.

In any case in which a defendant appeals his or her conviction because of some procedural error, and wins the appeal, the person may be re-tried, as long as no evidence that was ruled out because of the appeal is used. That is not double jeopardy. Miranda was re-tried, without using his confession, and was convicted of the same charges on the testimony of the victim. He was re-sentenced to two concurrent terms of twenty to thirty years.

That sentence did not mean that he would actually serve forty to sixty years. It just meant that he would not be paroled right away. Actually, he was paroled in 1972, and returned to his old haunts around Phoenix and Tempe, Arizona. One evening in July 1974, two Tempe police officers observed him driving around town. They stopped him and searched his car, and found a loaded handgun and drugs under the front seat. He was arrested and booked into jail, but no charges were filed because the prosecuting attorney found that the stop, search, and seizure were illegal. However, Miranda's parole agent was not held to the same legal standard as the police, and he had Miranda's parole revoked for possession of the gun and Miranda was returned to prison to resume serving his sentence.

Miranda was paroled again in April 1975, and again returned to his same old haunts. One evening in February 1976, while drinking beer in a barrio bar, he got into an argument with a young illegal Mexican who had just entered the country. He stabbed Miranda dead. The bar patrons held the illegal alien, while the bartender called the police.

When the police arrived, the officers recognized Miranda. They searched his pockets and found several cards with the *Miranda* warning printed on them; cards that he was known to sell near the Maricopa County court buildings. In a touch of irony, one officer stood the suspect against the bar, stood over the dead body of Ernesto Miranda, and read the suspect his rights from one of the cards taken from Miranda's pocket.

The Meaning of Miranda

Our system of justice is called an **adversary system**, because two sides (prosecution and defense) contest against each other in open court, similar to the knights' practice of trial by battle in early England. In theory, the legal truth will emerge from their contest. According to the Supreme Court Justices, the privilege against self-incrimination that is guaranteed in the Fifth Amendment shares a similar historical development from England, and is:

> …the essential mainstay of our adversary system, and guarantees to the individual the right to remain silent unless he chooses to speak in the unfettered exercise of his own will, during a period of custodial interrogation, as well as in the courts or during the course of other relevant investigations.

In its reasoning for the *Miranda* decision, the court explained that when a person is held in custody by law enforcement officers:

> …the atmosphere and environment of incommunicado interrogation as it exists today is inherently intimidating and works to undermine the privilege against self-incrimination.   Unless adequate preventive measures are taken to dispel the compulsion inherent in custodial surroundings, no statement obtained from the defendant can truly be the product of his free choice.

The purpose of the Supreme Court in requiring police to advise an arrested person of his or her rights before questioning was again **to "police the police."** It is similar to the *Mapp* decision in that the Warren Court did not trust the police or what they would do to obtain a confession and conviction. Warren had been a strong law-and-order district attorney in Alameda County, California, and later attorney general, where he had first-hand experience with what he could expect of overzealous police officers. Those experiences influenced his thinking and the decisions of the court.

The so-called *Miranda* warning was suggested by the court as a guideline to follow in providing the acceptable "**preventive measures**" required. Its specific wording was not required.

The only requirement is that police provide sufficient procedural safeguards to satisfy the court that a citizen's knowledge of his or her Fifth and Sixth Amendment rights and protection against self-incrimination are assured when a citizen is in custody and is about to be interrogated by police (hereinafter called **custodial interrogation**).

Not *Mirandizing* a person in custodial interrogation does not necessarily violate his or her constitutional rights. A person's rights are violated if a person's statements (confession) made without being advised, or otherwise given involuntarily, are admitted as evidence in what is called the prosecutor's case-in-chief, the prosecution's side of the case during the trial (***U.S. v. Verdugo-Urquidez,*** **1990**

Until recently, the actual *Miranda* warning was not considered to be a constitutional right. No civil liability would attach to an officer for interrogation of a suspect without giving the *Miranda* warning (***Brock v. Logan County,*** **1993**).

In a recent case, however, a majority of the U. S. Supreme Court held that **Miranda, itself, is a "constitutional rule"** (***Dickerson v. U. S.,*** **2000**). In addition, the Ninth Circuit Court of Appeals ruled in 1999 (***California Attorneys v. Butts***) that there were **possible civil rights violations** when two officers continued to interrogate two murder suspects after they had invoked their right to counsel and/or to silence. The officers also made false statements by telling the suspects that nothing they said could be used in court.

The requirement to admonish an adult suspect of the *Miranda* warning has been so distorted by its use in *cop* shows on television and in the movies that it is misunderstood by the general public and by some criminal justice personnel as well. Suspects usually are not *Mirandized* immediately upon arrest.

Miranda must be given only when two specific conditions are present at the same time:

> ➤ when a suspect is taken into custody, or otherwise deprived of freedom in a significant way

> ➤ if and when the person is subject to questioning as a suspect by a police officer about a crime

These two conditions are the **elements of custodial interrogation**. Also, the suspect must know that the person questioning him or her is a law enforcement officer. If the person is not in custody, and knows that he or she is free to leave, Miranda need not be given before questioning by police. Also, if the suspect is in custody but police do not question him or her, *Miranda* need not be given (see the Sixth Circuit Court of Appeals decision, **U.S. v. Salvo, 1998**, and the Ninth Circuit Court of Appeals decision, **Bains v. Cambra, 2000**).

The phrase "deprived of freedom in a significant way," means that the person is not free to leave and is restrained in freedom of movement, such as being cuffed and caged in a car, or locked in a room at the station (**CA v. Beheler, 1983**).

In the original *Miranda* decision, the court also stated that if the suspect indicates, prior to or during questioning, that he or she wishes to remain silent, the interrogation must cease. If he or she indicates that he or she wants an attorney, the interrogation must cease, and may not resume unless and until the attorney gives permission and is present during any questioning.

If the suspect does not make a clear invocation of his or her right to remain silent and to have an attorney, and merely asks the interrogating officers about the rights and/or if he or she should have an attorney, the officers must "...stop the interview and make a good-faith effort to give a simple and straightforward answer" (see *Almeida v. Florida,* 1999 and Florida *v. Glatzmayer,* **2001**).

When a suspect makes some statements without waiving his or her rights, **the suspect may stop** answering questions and **invoke his or her privilege** against self-incrimination or right to an attorney **at any time** during the interrogation. However, if the suspect does waive his or her rights, the waiver may be stated or implied in the responses to the *Miranda* admonition made by the suspect. That is, the suspect need not actually state that he or she waives his or her rights. He or she may imply a legal waiver by merely responding to a police officer's questions after being advised of the *Miranda* admonition (**North Carolina v. Butler, 1979**).

A **person's right to counsel**, as guaranteed in the Sixth Amendment, attaches to the person only after he or she has been formally charged in court and becomes the defendant in a criminal action. Therefore, the police do not provide an attorney if a person requests one after being *Mirandized*. The police must stop any efforts to interrogate the suspect. However, after an attorney has been hired or appointed by the court, after formally charging the defendant, the attorney's representation **is case-specific** (*McNeil v. Wisconsin*, **1991** and *Texas v. Cobb*, **2001**).

This means that while police may not question the suspect on the **instant offense** without the presence of an attorney, they may question him or her on other **unrelated offenses** for which he or she is not represented by an attorney, provided that they *Mirandized* the person on these unrelated offenses and obtained a waiver.

The Beheler Admonition

Many law enforcement agencies have a policy that the arresting officer is not to question the suspect about the crime. The officer merely effects the arrest and transports the person to jail. Consequently, no *Miranda* warning is required. If the suspect voluntarily offers incriminating information as to his or her role in the crime, it is admissible in court. Any *Mirandizing* will be done by the detectives investigating the case, and they will usually videotape, or at least audiotape, the officers giving the warning.

When a suspect has not been arrested, it is a common practice for investigative officers to ask a suspect if he or she would mind coming to police headquarters to discuss a matter. When the suspect arrives, he or she is given what is termed the **Beheler Admonition** or warning (*California v. Beheler*, **1983**), which goes something like the following:

> ➤ Thank you for coming down to the station. We want you to know that you are not under arrest, and that you are free to leave at any time. We just want to talk to you about a matter. Do you mind answering a few questions?

This creates a **consensual encounter**. It does not constitute custodial interrogation because the suspect is not under any restraint and is free to leave. It is in a sense a **consent interrogation**. Then, if a confession or incriminating statements are obtained, they are legally admissible. Even if the suspect does confess, he or she is still free to leave the station at any time. However, after he or she leaves, the officers will obtain an arrest warrant, using the confession as probable cause, and will arrest the suspect.

Miranda in Juvenile Cases

All the above information on *Miranda* applies only when the suspect is an adult at the time of arrest. Juvenile procedures have more rigorous requirements, because of a concept known as **independent state grounds**, discussed in Chapter 2. A state's legislature may enact laws providing greater protection for a person than the minimum required by the Constitution. California juvenile law (§625 WIC) requires an officer to advise a minor of his or her rights after taking a minor into temporary custody, **regardless of what disposition the officer intends to make**. However, there is no requirement to advise or even contact an adult prior to questioning a minor.

By way of information, many other states have additional procedural requirements for juveniles, called **interested adult laws that** require the advisement and/or consent of any waiver of Fifth and Sixth Amendment rights by some adult having a concern in the minor's welfare. Ohio, for example, requires consultation with an interested adult by the minor before questioning. In Indiana, legislation requires the consent of either the custodial parent, guardian, or attorney before a juvenile's rights may be waived.

In Connecticut, the Court of Appeals suppressed a juvenile's confession that was first made out of the presence of the father, and then repeated with the father present, after both the father and the minor had signed a waiver. Both minor and parent must be advised before any questioning may begin.

In Massachusetts, minors under the age of fourteen years must consult with an interested adult before waiving any rights, while minors fourteen and older must be advised and given the opportunity to consult with an interested adult. Georgia law requires merely that a minor's parents be advised upon taking a minor into custody, and allowed to consult if a request is made by the parent.

Procedures in New Hampshire follow the *totality of the circumstances*. However, it has a list of fifteen factors that must be considered in determining the legality of any waiver. Georgia has a 9-factor list. North Dakota statutes and appellate decisions require that an attorney be appointed for any minor not represented by a parent or guardian, and hold that a minor absolutely cannot waive his or her rights. Only an attorney, parents, or guardian can initiate a waiver.

In Oregon, police must *Mirandize* a juvenile, exactly as they would an adult. Police must also advise the parents before questioning the minor, and the parents or the minor may invoke the minor's Fifth and Sixth Amendment protections. However, if the minor is on probation as a ward of the court, the court may waive the minor's rights (as the substitute and legal parent), and then police are not required to advise the natural parents.

Nevada seems to provide juveniles with the most protection. There, police must advise the juvenile and the parent of the minor's *Miranda* rights, and both must waive the rights before questioning. In addition, if the minor is of an age, and has committed the type of offense that may allow for his or her waiver of jurisdiction to adult court to stand trial, police must advise him or her that anything the minor says may be used against him or her in criminal proceedings as an adult.

This extra protection for juveniles is not constitutionally necessary. Actually, the U. S. Supreme Court has held that the Miranda requirement is the same for juveniles (***In re Gault,*** **1967**, and ***Fare v. Michael C.,*** **1979**).

Miranda in Federal Juvenile Cases

Section 5033 of Title 18 of the United States Code (USC) prescribes the procedures that federal law enforcement officers must follow when taking a juvenile into custody.

> Whenever a juvenile is taken into custody for an alleged act of juvenile delinquency, the arresting officer **shall immediately advise** such **juvenile** of his legal rights, in language comprehensible to a juvenile, and shall immediately notify the Attorney General **and** the juvenile's **parents**, guardian, or custodian of such custody. The arresting officer **shall also notify the parents**, guardian, or custodian of the rights of the juvenile and of the nature of the alleged offense.

Federal law, then, provides far greater protection for juveniles than is required under *Miranda*, or any state. This federal requirement was reaffirmed by the U.S. Ninth Circuit Court of Appeals in their decision ***U.S. v. Rudolfo R.,*** **2000**.

The Sixth Amendment and the Right to Counsel Cases

Role of a Defense Attorney

A defense attorney does not defend what his or her client did, nor what the client is accused of doing. In fact, the criminal charge against the accused is irrelevant to the responsibility of the defense attorney. He or she **defends the constitutional rights** of an accused person because **every person** has these rights. That was one purpose in writing the Constitution in the first place, to protect citizens against government actions that might illegally deprive them of their freedom.

In protecting the accused, it is the responsibility of the defense attorney to be certain that all the actions of the police, the court, and correctional personnel are legal. That is why attorneys challenge the conduct of the police officer in every arrest and search, to test the legality of official conduct. This is the perspective taken by any good defense attorney. It is the only way he or she can do an effective job.

Every person accused of a crime has always had the right to an attorney if he or she could afford one. But it is only recently that those who could not afford an attorney actually received the assistance of counsel.

It took over thirty years, beginning in 1932, and several appellate decisions of the United States Supreme Court, to ensure that those who could not afford an attorney could have one appointed. The discussion below first reviews four appellate cases which created the right of indigents to appointed counsel.

The Scottsboro Boys

On March 25, 1931, nine young black men, ages 13 to 21 years, seven young white men, and two young white women were riding in the same freight car traveling across Alabama, when a fight broke out and the white men were thrown off the train.

They immediately notified the local sheriff, and, in addition to their assaults, claimed that the two white girls had been raped. The train was stopped by a sheriff's *posse* in the small town of Paint Rock, Alabama, and the young black men were arrested. When mob violence seemed imminent, the National Guard was summoned for protection and sheriff's deputies loaded the nine men onto a flatbed truck and moved them to the Jackson County jail in Scottsboro, Alabama.

There, the nine uneducated, poor, illiterate men were tried for the capital offense of rape, without the assistance of adequate counsel. On the first day of the trial, the judge did appoint a local lawyer, Milo Moody, to assist in their defense, but he had no preparation for the case. The nine were tried in groups of three, and it took three days to try and convict eight of the nine, even though medical testimony contradicted the girls' claims of rape. The judge declared a mistrial in the case of the ninth boy, the 13-year-old. The eight convicted men, known as the Scottsboro Boys, were sentenced to death.

Their case immediately made national headlines and motivated several defense attorney organizations to step in on behalf of the convicted men. On appeal, their convictions were reversed (***Powell v. Alabama, 1932***), and the Supreme Court ruled that **an indigent is entitled to the appointment of free counsel in capital cases**. This was the first precedent to be set on the right to counsel.

The case was set for re-trial in March 1933, with the assistance of counsel. The trials lasted over five years because of a number of legal motions and complications. In the meantime, all nine men remained in the Jackson County jail. Finally, charges were dropped against five of the nine. The other four were tried, convicted, and sentenced to life in prison. Eventually, three were paroled and one escaped.

Years later, one of the girls recanted her story and admitted that it was a lie. The second girl went to her grave without changing her story. The Scottsboro Boys eventually were pardoned by Governor Wallace of Alabama, although not all were living at the time.

The Betts Case

In 1941, an out-of-work farm hand on county relief, named Betts, was indicted for robbery in the Circuit Court of Carroll County, Maryland. He was unable to afford an attorney, so he requested that counsel be appointed for him at arraignment. The judge denied his request and said that it was not the practice in Carroll County to appoint counsel for indigent defendants, except in prosecutions of capital cases.

Without waiving his asserted right to counsel, Betts pleaded not guilty and asked to be tried without a jury. At his request, witnesses were summoned on his behalf. Betts cross-examined the state's witnesses and examined his own witnesses. His witnesses gave testimony tending to establish an alibi. Although afforded the opportunity, Betts did not take the witness stand. The judge found him guilty, and imposed a sentence of eight years.

He appealed, alleging that he had been deprived of the right to assistance of counsel guaranteed by the Sixth Amendment by virtue of the Fourteenth Amendment.   His appeal was denied all the way through the state's appellate system and up to the U. S. Supreme Court. Justice Roberts issued the Supreme Court's opinion on June 1, 1942 (***Betts v. Brady*, 1942**). The court held that:

> The Sixth Amendment of the national Constitution applies only to trials in federal courts. The due process clause of the Fourteenth Amendment does not incorporate, as such, the specific guarantees found in the Sixth Amendment...

Thus, Betts's conviction was upheld and he remained in prison to serve his sentence. Precedent was set by this case. Indigents accused of felonies in state courts did not have a constitutional right to appointed counsel, unless some **special circumstances** about the case, such as illiteracy or mental incompetence, would make self-representation unfair.

For the next twenty years, thousands of indigent defendants were convicted without the assistance of counsel and were sent to prison. Every time a conviction was appealed, the Supreme Court referred to *Betts* as precedent, and had to look for special circumstances if a conviction was to be reversed.

The Gideon Case

In 1963, the U. S. Supreme Court did an unusual thing. It completely reversed itself on the *Betts* precedent in the case of ***Gideon v. Wainwright***.

In 1960, Clarence Earl Gideon, a 48-year old itinerant laborer from Hannibal, Missouri, was arrested and charged with breaking into the Bay Harbor Pool Room in Panama City, Florida, and stealing about $65 out of the coin-operated machines, as well as some beer, wine, and Coca-Cola. The charge was felony burglary. He requested an attorney, but the trial judge, Robert L. McCrary, Jr., refused, based on existing practice and precedent. Gideon attempted to defend himself against the skills of prosecutor Bill Harris, but he was convicted and sentenced to a term of five years at the Union Correctional Institution in Raiford. Gideon appealed to the U. S. Supreme Court, in his own hand-written petition, with the help of Joe Peel, a former lawyer and city judge who was in Raiford serving time on a murder conviction.

The Supreme Court heard the case and announced its unanimous opinion on March 18, 1963 *(Gideon v. Wainwright, 1963)*. Justice Black wrote the opinion, stating that:

> The right of one charged with crime to counsel may not be deemed fundamental and essential to fair trials in some countries, but it is in ours. From the very beginning, our state and national constitutions and laws have laid great emphasis on procedural and substantive safeguards designed to assure fair trials before impartial tribunals in which every defendant stands equal before the law. This noble ideal cannot be realized if the poor man charged with crime has to face his accusers without a lawyer to assist him.

The Gideon decision made it mandatory that judges in state courts **appoint free counsel to indigents accused of felonies**. The Supreme Court stated that it "…was a fundamental right, essential to a fair trial." Using the wording of the Fourteenth Amendment, the Court made the binding on all the states.

Gideon's case was set for re-trial before the original court in Panama City. The prosecutor, Bill Harris, offered a plea bargain whereby Gideon would plead guilty to the charge in return for a sentence of time served. His defense attorney, a local lawyer appointed to represent him named W. Fred Turner, suggested that he take the deal. Gideon refused and demanded a jury trial. With the assistance of Mr. Turner, he was found not guilty and the charges were dismissed. In fact, the testimony at the second trial showed that Gideon might have been framed by the man who testified at the first trial, Henry Cook, who claimed to have seen Gideon in the pool room when it was burglarized (*Daily Journal*, p. 22).

The Gideon decision was made **retroactive**, which meant that it applied to all past cases. The officials in every state had to review their prison records to determine who had been convicted without the help of an attorney. Anyone so convicted, and there were thousands, had to be either re-tried or released.

Gideon had one more brush with the law. He was arrested for vagrancy in Kentucky in 1965, claiming he had lost all his money on the Kentucky Derby. He spent one night in jail. He died in poverty, and as a family outcast, on January 18, 1972. He was buried in a pauper's grave with a wooden marker, in Hannibal, Missouri, and not even the remaining members of his family who lived there attended his funeral.

Ten years later, members of the American Civil Liberties Union (ACLU) felt that Gideon had made such a contribution to the livelihood of so many lawyers that on the tenth anniversary of his death, they collected funds from attorneys nation-wide, erected a marble headstone at his grave site and held a belated funeral service commemorating his contribution.

Many thought that the Gideon decision meant that anyone charged with a crime could have free counsel, but it actually included only accused felons.

The Argersinger Case

In 1969, another indigent in Florida, named Argersinger, was arrested and charged with possession of a concealable firearm, a misdemeanor punishable by a jail term of up to six months or a $1,000 fine. He was not informed of the right to an attorney at arraignment, and he pled guilty. He was given a 90-day jail sentence. He appealed his conviction, claiming that he had been denied his Sixth Amendment right to an attorney, even though he was released long before the appeal was ever argued. Justice Douglas wrote the Supreme Court's opinion (*Argersinger v. Hamlin,* **1972**), which was released on June 12, 1972, and stated that:

> The right of an indigent defendant in a criminal trial to the assistance of counsel, which is guaranteed by the Sixth Amendment as made applicable to the States by the Fourteenth, is not governed by the classification of the offense or by whether or not a jury trial is required. **No accused may be deprived of his liberty as the result of any criminal prosecution, whether felony or misdemeanor, in which he was denied the assistance of counsel.**

The assistance of counsel, a right that people today take for granted, has only been in practice for felons in all the states since 1963, by *Gideon*, and finally in

1972, for all defendants who stand to lose their freedom, by *Argersinger*. That is not very long ago.

Those decisions not only gave indigents a new constitutional protection and released many convicted inmates from prisons and jails; they also created an immediate need for states to establish public defender systems and other appointed counsel methods.

Summary

This monograph gave a brief history of the development of criminal court procedure and then examined two procedural rules, the *Exclusionary Rule* and the *Miranda Warning,* that made the Fourth, Fifth and Sixth Amendment guarantees of the Bill of Rights available to all individuals suspected of crimes.

The *Weeks'* case initially created the rule known as the *Weeks Doctrine*, but it applied only in federal court cases. In the 1949 *Wolf* case, the Court specifically declined to extend that protection to state courts and make it binding on local law enforcement. Finally, in 1961, the *Mapp* case was used as a vehicle by the Supreme Court to apply the Exclusionary rule to all the states, and local law enforcement officers have had to comply with it in the collection of any evidence, whether that evidence is physical or testimonial. The *Mapp* case was decided by a due-process-oriented court, headed by Chief Justice Earl Warren, whose concern for fairness and individual rights was paramount.

Three exceptions to the rule also have been created through the *Williams*, *Quarles*, and *Leon* cases. This is due primarily to the appointments of an increasing number of Supreme Court Justices with a more law-and-order orientation than those before them. This includes Chief Justice Warren Burger, followed by Chief Justice Rehnquist, both of whom had hoped to lead the court back to the right and reverse the liberal due process oriented procedures established under Chief Justice Earl Warren, and thereby fulfilling the plans of Presidents Nixon, Reagan and Bush, whose appointments to the court were intended to facilitate that reversal (Simon, 1995). Burger almost succeeded in convincing a majority of the justices to overturn *Mapp*, but his persuasive powers were not quite strong enough (Woodward & Armstrong, 1979, pp. 112-121).

With regard to Miranda, the defining concept is known as *custodial interrogation*, the questioning of a suspect in custody or under similar restraints about his or her role in a crime. Several case situations that were forerunners of the *Miranda* decision also were discussed: the *McNabb* and *Mallory* requirement of *prompt arraignment*, and the *Escobedo* requirement of on-the-spot counsel. The use of what is known as the *Beheler Admonition* was described as a contemporary approach to questioning suspects without arresting them.

The final portion of this monograph examined the role of a defense attorney, along with four appellate cases, Betts, Gideon, and Argersinger, that extended the Sixth Amendment right to counsel to every accused individual so that, in theory, everyone stands equal before the law.

References

Bray, Zack, "Appellate Review and the Exclusionary Rule," *Yale Law Review*, Mar. 2004, b. 113, No. 5, p. 1143.

Cavin, Jeffery D. "Waiver of a Juvenile's Fifth and Sixth Amendment Rights," *Journal of Juvenile Law*, Vol. 13, 1992, pp. 27-41.

Carter, Dan T. *Scottsboro: A Tragedy of the American South*, 2nd ed. Baton Rouge: Louisiana University Press, 1984

Colb, Sherry, "A World without Privacy: Why Property Does Not Define the Limits of the Right Against Unreasonable Searches and Seizures," *Michigan Law Review*, Mar. 2004, v. 102, No. 5, p. 990.

Kamisar, Yale, "The Exclusionary Rule in Historical Perspective: The Struggle to Make the Fourth Amendment More Than an Empty Blessing", *Judicature* (November 1978)

Lewis, Anthony. *The Supreme Court and How It Works: The Story of the Guideon Case.* New York: Random House, 1966

Rothwax, Judge Harold J. *The Collapse of Criminal Justice.* New York: Random House, 1996.

Scheb, John M. & John M. Scheb II. *Criminal Procedures*, Belmont, CA: Wadsworth, 1999.

Simon, James F. *The Center Holds: The Poser Struggle Inside the Rehnquist Court.* New York: Simon & Schuster, 1995.

Sherrow, Victoria. *Gideon v. Wainwright: Free Legal Counsel (Landmark Court Cases).* Berkeley Heights, NJ: Enstow Publishers, 1995.

Tushnet, Mark. *A Court Divided: The Rehnquist Court and the Future of Constitutional Law*, New York: W. W. Norton, 2005

Wice, Paul B. *Gideon v. Wainwright and the Right to Counsel.* Danbury, CT: Franklin Watts, 1995.

Woodward, Bob and Scott Armstrong. *The Brethren: Inside the Supreme Court.* New York: Simon & Schuster, 1979.

Appellate Cases

Adams v. United States, 317 US 269 (1942)

Almeida v. Florida, 737 So, 2nd 520 (1999)

Argersinger v. Hamlin, 407 U.S. 25 (1972)

Arizona v. Evans, 514 U.S. 1 (1996)

Bains v. Cambra, 98-17223 2000)

Betts v Brady, U.S. 445 (1942)

Brewer V. Williams, 430 U. S. 387 (1977)

Brock v. Logan County, 3 F3d 1215, 1217 (1993)

California Attorneys v. Butts 195 F.3d 1039 (1999)

California v. Beheler, 463 U.S. 1121 (1983)

Dickerson v. U.S., 530 U.S. 99-5525 (2000)

Duckworth v. Eagan, 492 U.S. 195 (1989)

Edwards v. Arizona, 451 U.S. 477 (1981)

Escobedo v. Illinois, 378 U.S. 478 (1964)

Fare v. Michael C., 442 U.S. 707 (1979)

Gideon v. Wainwright, 372 U.S. 335 (1963)

Florida v. Glatzmayer, No. SCoo-602 (2001)

Illinois v. Krull, 480 U.S.340 (1987)

In re Gault, 387 U. S. 1 (1967)

In re Jensen Cal.App.4th No. D036480 (2001)

McNabb v. U. S., 318 U. S. 332 (1943)

McNeil v. Wisconsin, 501 U.S. 171 (1991)

Mallory v. U. S., 354 U. S. 449 (1957)

Mapp v Ohio, 367 U. S 643 (1961)

McKaskle v. Wiggins, 79 L.Ed 2d 122 (1984)

Michigan v. Tucker, 417 U.S. 433 (1974)

Miranda v. Arizona, 384 U.S. 444 (1966)

Moran v. Burbine, 475 U.S. 412 (1986)

New York v. Quarles, 467 U.S. 649 (1984)

Nix v. Williams, 467 U. S. 431 (1984)

North Carolina v. Butler, 441 U.S. 369 (1979)

Powell v. Alabama, 287 U.S. 45 (1932)

State v. Williams, 182 N. W. 2d 396 (1970)

Texas v. Cobb, 121 S. Ct. 1335 (2001)

U. S. v. Brady, 819 F. 2d 884 (9th DCA 1987)

U. S. v. DeSantis, 870 F. 20 536 (9th DCA 1989)

U. S. v. Carrillo, 16 F. 3d 1046 (9th DCA 1994)

U.S. v. Leon, 468 U. S. 897 (1984)

U. S. v. McLaughlin, 931 F. 2d 898 (1988)

U.S. v. Salvo, 133 F.3d 943 (1998)

U. S. v. Verdugo-Urquidez, 494 U. S. 259 (1990)

Weeks v. U.S., 232 U.S.383 (1914)

Wolf v. Colorado, 338 U. S. 25, (1949)

* 9 7 8 0 9 8 3 5 0 4 9 3 1 *